What I Gave You

What I Gave You

Madison Kelley

Illustrations by Konstantin Bessmertny

New Degree Press
Copyright © 2021 Madison Kelley
All rights reserved.

What I Gave You

ISBN   978-1-63730-714-4   Paperback
         978-1-63730-852-3   Kindle Ebook
         979-8-88504-001-3   Ebook

Contents

Note from the Author   11
What I Gave You   15

Part 1. The Departure   17
Rapunzel   18
Battleground   19
Clouds   22
Château Margaux   24
Maybe / Why   26
The Chasm   28
Lockdown   29
The Traveler   31
The Ascent   33
The Last Garden in Macau   34
it's lonely in the middle   37
To all the witches: 39
Fluent   42
A Good Girl   43
One-Sided   45
Kousei's Story   47
Janie's Story   49
The Storm   52

Part 2. Turbulence   53
The Whole Package   54
Peonies on the Dining Table   55
Valentine's Day   56

Rhode Island	58
Dirty	60
February 8th	62
My Favorite Lie	64
To Send You a Text	65
Happy Birthday	67
Paper Plane	68
Golden	70
A Cold Night in Paris	71
Forgive Me	73
All the Problems	74
San Francisco	75
Light On	77
Ribbon Around My Wrist	78
Angel	80
Knotted	82
Middle Ground	83
Train Wreck	85
Alice's Story	86
I'm the worst, but you knew that	90
Solo Date	92
Toothpaste	94
The Castle	95
Atlas Buckled at the Knee	97
Jack-in-the-box	98
Geppetto	100
Magnetic Properties	102
Drunk	103
Allison's Story	104
Antidote	107

Part 3. The Arrival	**109**
The Difference	110
Celeste	111
Petals of My Past	112
Daffodil	114
Puddles	115
January	116
Faith	118
The Art of Performing	120
Golden Hour	122
If I Could Build a Man	123
Charlotte's Story	125
Paradise	133
I Met Fate and He Wore Red	135
My Love Affair with the Sun	137
Plot the Course	138
The Precipice	140
Landscape in Ink	142
My Greatest Fear	143
Confidante	145
Garden Walk	146
Imposter	148
My Truth	149
Dear Maddie,	150
Acknowledgments	153

You gave me everything. This is the last thing I can give you.

Note from the Author

I think we can all agree that 2020 wasn't the greatest year. Though, somehow, I found freedom.

In 2019, I moved from sunny California to Macau for an exciting work opportunity. Little did I know, I would get trapped here during a global pandemic. When lockdown first started in early March, everything seemed fine, like it couldn't last forever. Macau closed its borders to travelers to contain the virus. When March turned to April, I started to get angry. I had to cancel a trip to Japan, and as April turned to June, I was living in a haze of negative emotions. Being sequestered on this tiny island was making me crazy. I'm sure all of you can relate, but I had no outlet to express this bubbling frustration towards a situation I had no control over, but nonetheless exerted complete control over me. Writing became my only release.

I would stumble upon moments in which I would see the sentences forming in front of me, and I would have to stop everything to write them down. This was a different experience than I'd ever had before. Apart from my usual journaling in college, I searched for inspiration and forced myself to squeeze out something artsy. But during the pandemic, I experienced inspiration as a slap in the face, almost as if my subconscious was urging me to deal with the situation by writing. Each time I furiously typed the words, I would feel the most cathartic release. I wanted to tell stories, not just about myself but about people in general. I am a zealous fiction reader and an avid anime fan, so a lot of my inspiration comes from Saturday nights in bed consuming stories. Being in isolation strangely gave me the space to dream, to rewrite my reality, and imagine a world in which things were different. I started seeing incredibly vivid scenes in my head. A cold rainy night, a lonely diner on the side of a highway, headlights and a neon sign. A brown-haired, brown-eyed, plain looking waitress, serving coffee. Immediately I knew every detail about her, and I had to tell her story. You'll meet Allison later.

This collection is a journey, with a clear beginning, middle, and end, with characters that I hope you can relate to and even find yourself rooting for. As such, I took great care in ensuring that I present my readers with not just a cohesive narrative, but also a story that captures your heart. The beginning, Part 1, represents the departure. Leaving home for the first time and coming to terms with who you are, especially the parts you don't want to face. Part 2 details the experience of being completely engrossed in someone else and the high that comes with first love. But what comes up must come back down, and heartbreak is a lot like turbulence. It feels like the plane is going to crash, but eventually you'll land safely on the ground. This brings us to Part 3: the arrival. You've learned more about yourself, and more importantly, who you want to be. It feels like you finally know which direction to point your compass. My greatest hope for this book is that you can read it and relate in some small way. If it helps you feel seen, or helps you move on from a situation, then I couldn't ask for anything more. In my own life, I'm at Part 3. I am confident in the steps that I am taking towards my future, and I can't wait to see what lies ahead. When you close the book, I hope you feel the same sense of serenity and settling.

But before you jump in, I want to ask you a question. Do you think poetry is boring? That it's not for you? If you answered yes, then thank you for getting this far into this note. However, you aren't alone—I thought that, too. The last time I read poetry was in high school and I was more worried about my grades than the poems. I found the ambiguity within the poems confusing and the overall narrative difficult to relate to. Nonetheless, I write poetry. "How can that be?" you might ask. In the highest moments of emotion, I write. I pour every ounce of anger or sadness or happiness that I'm feeling right then and there onto the page. Those five-, ten-, twenty-minute intervals when I'm letting myself feel are the stories you're about to read. For that reason, *What I Gave You* couldn't be anything other than a collection of poems. The title refers to the experiences that the universe gave me, but it also refers to what I'm giving to you. All of these moments starting in 2014, up to today, coming together to tell the story of being in your early twenties. First tastes of independence, first loves, first heartbreaks, and ultimately coming to a place of peace.

One where you can look back on what was and understand how it brought you to the precipice of your future.

So, my dear reader, are you ready? In anticipation of what is to come, I wanted to give you a little taste, an *amuse-bouche*, if you will.

What I Gave You

Delicate paper fastened with tape
Unwrap my words
And inside you'll find
What I gave you.

All of my heart.
The emotions I disavow
The love I reserve for a select few.

All of my fantasy.
The imaginary friends who live in my head
The places I wish to live when I grow up.

All of my fears.
The worry that I'll never be enough and
The times I ran from the hard choices.

This is my everything
All of my hopes and dreams
Realized and unrealized.

My lifeline
When my lungs could no longer process
The oxygen this world provides.

Be gentle with me.
But my greatest hope
Is that at the bottom of the box

You won't just find me
But yourself as well.

PART 1:

THE DEPARTURE

Rapunzel

With sunlight hair and summer sky eyes
Skilled at subverting her true sentiments
A shimmery façade boasts dazzling lies.
A proposal gilded in promises for the future:
Sparkly new job
Ostensibly capable of jumpstarting a career by years.
Up the tower
Locked the door
But kept the key.
She gazes out, longing for what was left behind:
Friends
Family
Love.
Just behind her was the exit.
Apathy sings a nauseatingly sweet melody,
"Rapunzel, Rapunzel let down your long hair."
    Not yet.
She accepted a commitment
Two-year solitary confinement of her own making.
This is supposed to be the right thing.

To protect herself from regret and heartache
She surrenders herself to the dream
That she never had a heart to begin with
Because lies taste so much better than the truth
When they're dripping with gold.

Battleground

Leave it to me to rip my own heart out and walk away saying, "Oh, that doesn't hurt at all, I'm totally fine. In fact, this is exactly what I wanted."

I have a special talent for convincing myself in situations like this that I'm not slowly bleeding out from loneliness. It's incredible, actually, how I can function having completely severed the link between my head and my heart.

> "Follow me! Heart is weak, governed by shit that's fleeting, intangible and incomprehensible. She doesn't even have strings! We can't rely on a liar like her, right?"

Well that's some logic I can't deny... right?

> "Yea, some fake ass logic made up by a Brain without a compass and a keen sense for stuffing 10 pounds of crap in a 5 pound jar.
> Screwing the lid on so tight it's about to crack the glass.
> *I'm* the one who feels when it leaks every now and again from all the pent-up guilt and regret we've decided we don't believe in.
> Good one Brain,
> very prudent of you,
> excellent survival mechanisms."

And what's left?

A girl who runs from feelings and people, apt at telling ourselves lies to make it okay?

> "*You* might have severed the link
> but *I* still hear Brain's whispers.
> Her Machiavellian ambition
> consistently driving us into states of desolation.
> Gives me heartburn."

> "But, Heart's not much better! So selfish for trying to convince us to give up on a long-term goal to satisfy her 'current' needs! Real classy, Heart."

You're not helping either! Between your incessant howling and the Heart's eternal desire to ignore you, it's a marvel I'm not deaf from all the screaming matches.

But then again, if you two were actually able to come to some sort of compromise, would it really change anything anyway?

Wait which one of you is talking right now?

Which one am I?

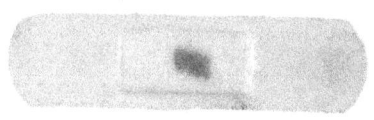

бинт, порезал

23.11.2012

Clouds

30,000 feet in the air
Looking out the window
Dreaming what it would be like
To land on a cloud.

Stay for a while and melt into it like cotton candy
Even jump up and down on it like a hotel bed.
After I get tired, I'll recline
Watch from above the world below
Alive and bustling.

People would go on drama full and drama free
But I would be up on the clouds.
No more fretting the tedious trivialities of humanity
My life would be different.

But that's impossible.
If I jumped out of this plane and tried to land on a cloud
I would fall right through
And land splat on the ground.

So I don't jump.
Stay safely in my seat.
Wait to land like everyone else.
Then shuffle out and go on living
The mass-produced American dream.

But I'll keep wishing
Until the day I'm put in the ground
That for one day
I could live among the clouds.

Château Margaux

Nose deep in this glass of wine.
Breathe in.
What do you feel?
Joy?
Do I smell a hint of passion fruit?
Sip.
Breathe out.
The lightness goes first
Followed by the slightest prick of dolor.
Leaving tears of deep red.
On my birthday today
I just want to feel some semblance of life.
But life isn't just one thing
It's not just good times
It's not just bad times
It's not consistent.
They say the grapes that grow in the harshest conditions
Make the sweetest wine.
Sadness and joy make the perfect blend
The ultimate balance.
This year was a good year.
Notes of sour cherries and rich blackberries
Uncharacteristically warm for a cold person.
Don't you taste that bitterness among all the sweet?

THE HERMIT

Sorrow can be alleviated by good sleep,
a bath and a glass of wine.

IX
THOMAS AQUINAS

Maybe / Why

Every time I get close
To settling down
I end up walking away.
I've lost count of
The many times
I've been head over heels happy,
Realized it,
And immediately turned left.

I run out of tracks
Trying to catch my train of thought
As to why I leave the people I love behind.
Why we all lead different lives.

Technology affords us the opportunity to be
Better friends
Better family.
So tell me why it's so hard to stay in touch.
Why I can't bring myself to pick up the phone.
Why I get anxious from the sound of a FaceTime dial.

At this point it feels like a crapshoot where I'll eventually end up.
I just hope that by that point
My nephew won't see me as a stranger.

My college friends taught me that
People make the place.

If I know this to be true
Then why do I keep chasing new cities?

Maybe I can only see things clearly from airplane windows
and foreign apartments.
Or maybe the universe could be better about throwing me
a bone every once in a while.
Maybe for once the good times could last longer,
So maybe I could spend Christmas with my
brother *and* my best friend.
Maybe we won't have to wait for each other's weddings
to reunite.
Maybe all my grandparents could live in the same town.

I miss you.

Maybe I just have a shitty personality
One that only grows under intense pressure
From being isolated.

Or maybe,
Just maybe,
There's beauty
In having left pieces of my heart
With each and every one of you.

The Chasm

I watch it all in slow motion. Everyone is standing in front of me. The sky is not blue but not gray. I'm in a desert with no landscape; no escape. Just the sand beneath my feet and the glass-like sky as the backdrop. Every important person in my life standing right in front of me. Behind me is this abyss, a bottomless chasm. I only shift my weight, but I feel the earth crumble beneath my foot. My heel slips, catching me off balance. I'm teetering backwards. I feel the emptiness on my back like a curtain. Everyone is blank. No one runs to grab my hand. No one says anything. *Why aren't I trying to brace my fall? Shouldn't falling be faster? Why isn't someone doing something?* Like running underwater, my limbs are fighting against time, fighting gravity. God says, "Watch what's happening, understand it. Recognize that you're the one who put yourself here.

This is a world of your making,

not mine."

Lockdown

April
The world went under water.
I'm exhausted from this constant treading
but I'm used to it.

Thought I found the lighthouse
A flash of hope that life was returning to normal
But it was just a buoy.
I was about to close my eyes
Drift to the bottom and be buried with the fish,
But I used what little I had left
To string together a life vest
Out of new friends and new projects.

Cool October embraced me
I'm settled now.
The leaves have fallen
To form a new me.
It's exciting.

But it's hard to be grateful when January is making me numb
I just want to see my family.
Holding onto hope so hard I'm losing feeling in my fingers
but I'm used to it.

No idea what February will bring.
Just gained my footing in this new way of life
Only to have the carpet ripped out from under me

Friends leaving
Relationships ending
but I'm used to it.

I found comfort living between
Glass half full and
Glass half empty.
Lost in the open ocean.
Safe
But alone.
Appreciative
But unhappy.
These waves make me nauseous.
I'm sick of being used to it.

So I bought all the clocks in this god forsaken place
Just to try to turn back time
To last year
When I could still see my friends.
One more dinner & drinks.

I should've stayed in California.

The Traveler

Like a traveler in the desert I stumbled upon the oasis
Into a world where even paupers could live like kings.
This tiny city makes life easy.
Work just enough for pay
Nothing more than 15 minutes away.
It's a dangerous haven for dreamers like me.

Prada bags and palatial apartments
Starting to outweigh the goals of
Moving to Burbank and building lands.
I used to know exactly what I wanted.
The girl I was before the move
Drank from her Imagineering mug every morning.
We were going to be the CEO someday.

My North Star blinks like a neon sign
The smoky bar clouds my judgement
I'm trying to keep my dreams in vision but,
This port is from 1886, so
Yes, I'll have another glass.
Sweet distraction warming my stomach
Goes down easy
Blurring my surroundings
That's how I like it.

Home is too quiet.
It's easier to lose myself in the moment
Than listen to her pleading

Telling me there's something we're meant to be doing
Other places we're meant to be going.

As the days turn into months
Suddenly another year has gone by.
Her pleas grow faint
Just whispers now

Don't lose your way

    Focus

        Remember

The Ascent

Looking up through the patchwork of leaves
Desperate to see the view from above the trees
I begin my ascent.
Maybe from up there I'll see the horizon.

Didn't feel the bark tear through my palm
Blood drops to the same beat as my heart
Frost bites at my toes
I cry out in frustration
Lightning cackles at my agony.

I fall asleep shivering from the September rain
Hoping I'll sleep through January.
But December is here and I watch it go by.
Trapped in this wood and sap labyrinth
The wind laughs at my feeble attempt to look ahead
Time blows away.

Unmoored from everything I used to know
Only the splinters in my fingertips anchor me to
the present.
I don't know what spring will look like
But the breeze is a gentle kiss on the cheek.
Growing comfortable in the unknown
I left all notions of normality in the leaves below.

The Last Garden in Macau

Staring down
today's
list
of
to-do
items.
I woke up early, 6:30
as usual,
put on my pot of tea and
enjoyed the papers on the veranda.
At 7:30 I showered and changed.
At 8:30 I walked across the street to my employer's home
donned my gloves and my tools
and prepared myself for another hot day.

    Another day.

How is it that the details are different
but the view's the same?
I prune the trees
I plant the flowers
I pull the weeds.
My labors are nurturing life
I can see the dirt under my fingernails,
I can feel the strain in my back at the end of the day,
but somehow,
for me
nothing's changed.

Wiping the sweat off my brow
the clouds are dark and imposing now.
I can smell the rain that is threatening to pour down.
I can feel the thunder getting ready to assert its presence.
And like my growing anxiety,
I wonder when it will reach its breaking point.

Another year has gone by
blink.
I've watched friends come and go
blink.
Before this garden
I was so free.
Drive up the coast,
fly to Paris,
no problem.
But, now
I'm tied to this land.
I want to go
but how
to where
to what?

The thought of yet another year
passing by
like dandelion seeds in the wind…

So I throw myself into the garden.
I make small re-designs

To keep moving.
If I were to stand still and watch
As the world around me keeps spinning,
I would crumble like the soil in my hands.

I don't know how else to express
That I don't have any control
That I'm stuck in the same place
Doing the same things.
Something that used to be inconceivable for an
independent woman who didn't grow roots.

All I can do is plant the seeds
in the last garden in Macau.

it's lonely in the middle

My whole life I wanted to be pretty
I wanted to be liked
I didn't want to be a Victoria's Secret Angel
I wouldn't ask for that much.
But just when I started to like myself
    I'm more alone than ever before.
Turned away like a Rolex priced at free.
Fifteen-year-old me who felt ugly next to a prize hog
Never imagined the price that came with
high cheekbones and clear skin.
But what's worse
A girl who loves herself?
    Or a girl who hates herself?

They say it's lonely at the top
    But I'm in the middle
Sandwiched between perfection and mediocrity.
Just below the tens who already have it locked down
But somehow surpassing the safe sixes.

Would you like me better if I shrank for you?
Would you not have to hold your boyfriend's hand
A little tighter
During dinner?
Would you trust me more if kept my distance?

You treat me like an accused witch
Guilty until proven a homewrecker.
Hold me in your hand and I'll shatter

Leaving my jagged edges pierced in your palm.
Do I look made of glass to you?

I want to be your friend, but
I'm thinking about just walking away.
Things were easier when I didn't leave my room.
I'm at my wits end of a lose-lose situation
I feel like a house of cards
With a gentle breeze on the horizon.

To all the witches:

Rise.
The wild at heart
The strong in thought.
Hear my cry
At midnight tonight
during the height
of the equinox.

I implore you
Sisters
Heed my plight
For I have stood
Where you stand
And
Felt the trembling
When faced with evil
At its core.

Fear not the warlocks
And demons
Anymore
For with this potion
In my heart
I gift you with
An antidote.

When they come
In the middle of the night
With poisons

That render you weak
Fear not.

When they say
No one will believe
Your tears and
With their magic
Turn truth
Into the sweetest of lies
Fear not.

When their hordes
And clans
Spit venom in your face
Fear not.

Because
You
Are not
Alone.

You come from a line
Of witches
Who paved the way
With calloused hands
And throbbing feet
To build this pedestal
For us
To fight.

Together
We take
Our broomsticks
Our spells
Our voices
To boom the echo
Of generations
Of women
Who fought
For their daughters'
Better life.

Together
We take back
This endless night.

Fluent

"You took something from my desk without asking."

For the third time this week.

"You're being dramatic,"
He said.

Insert eye roll here.

Since I'm now fluent in mansplaining,
allow me to translate:

"I know what I did was wrong,
but I'm too insecure to admit it."

A Good Girl

Listens
Smiles
Always wins a lose-lose
Is non-threatening.

She holds her head high
Strong
Even when someone overpowers her
Because it's her fault anyway.

You were drunk, right?
You can't remember anyway, right?
Of course she was in the wrong.

A lesson I learned
A bit too late
A good girl
Is not worth the weight of her halo.

The fear of not being believed
Is a master of bondage
Tying me to the smallest version of myself.

I am learning
Every day
How to untie the knots.

My fight will not end
With pretty words on perishable paper.
I will teach my daughters
As my mother taught me

I am the only one
Who determines
Who I am.

One-Sided

Such a beautiful fool
Letting you lead me around the ring like a tamed lion
You were the center of my circus.
I signed the contract fully aware of what lied
between the lines
The lies I told myself
Your brutal honesty.
I thought I was the star of your show
I thought if I followed your instructions
We could be more.

The first time you broke my heart
In the parking lot of the Suncoast Casino
I cried all the way home.
Listening to your words on repeat
    "I can't see you anymore."
I barely saw the stoplights between tears.

But I was a well-trained circus animal.
You let me out of my cage once
And I came running back the first chance I got.
Convinced myself that you felt the same
That it couldn't have just been me
Who didn't care about texts
From anyone else.

But sitting in your car at 7/11
    "So we're just friends right?"

That cherry Slurpee tasted like dirt as
You buried me in my own delusion.

I'm sorry for hating you for so long
I swear I've grown since then.
You were nothing but honest with me and
I refused to believe it
Since we both knew that your hand in mine
Felt so right.

I don't love you anymore
But I think a piece of me still wants to.
To this day I still wonder what you felt.
Was it really one-sided?
All this time I've been holding onto the ropes
Trying to keep the big top tent from blowing away
Because I never got a proper goodbye.

I think it would be enough for me to let go
If I knew that you were happy now
That you don't have any regrets
That you don't wonder what could've been
That you don't even remember my name.

Kousei's Story

I thought about you today
Like I do every day.
You took needle and thread
And sewed your name into every inch of me.

I'm walking through the park where we first met.
Twelve years to the day.
Are you watching?
Up above the world so high
My tears like shooting stars.

I wish you had been honest,
That your cough wasn't just a cold.
Although,
It wouldn't have changed the fact that
You broke down the door
And made yourself at home in my heart.
Running my fingers over the scars you left me with
I smile despite the reminder that you're not here.
The most beautiful pain
Even now, all these years later.

Greedy me,
I'm dreaming again
Of chasing after you
Your talent and your love of the violin
My lungs on fire, fighting just to catch up.
But,
Those slow afternoons in the music room

After you brought me back to the piano
My world filled with melody.

I'll never forget that day in January
Being your accompanist
The hand helping your beauty shine.
Outside the snow fell in every shade of you and
I knew I wanted to accompany you forever.

But then,
Just like those snowflakes
You melted before I got the chance to see you in detail.
I guess you knew from the beginning
That you wouldn't be around for the fall.
Surrounded by yellows and orange
All I felt was red.
You left me to play alone.

I will always wish to play together one more time
But once you meet someone you're never alone.
I still hear your voice in the cherry blossom petals
I see your blonde hair in the sunny summer breeze.
Walking by your parents' bakery for canelés
I breathe in the sweet scent of you each winter.

Spring is just around the corner,
And though I'm without you again,
I'm so thankful for that lie you told in April.

Janie's Story

>   Janie,
>   Do you remember when
>   We broke into that old house
>   To watch the sunset from the attic?
>   We ran from the cops so fast I thought we were floating.
>   I can still hear your laughter
>   When whiskey makes me dizzy.
>   I'm sure you look down on me
>   For staying in this little town
>   Taking over Pop's place.
>   But it's all I've ever known,
>   And walking down Main Street is the only place I can
>   Feel you anymore.
>   Looking at your Instagram I don't recognize you,
>   You're always someplace new.

James,
Why don't you update your stories?
Seriously,
How else am I supposed to know what you're up to?
I wish
I could say I regret leaving
But my imagination could never fit in New Castle.
If you asked how I was
I'd say I was great,
That I got everything I wanted.
Nobody thought I could make it as a blogger in New York.
Now,
Work is so busy

I can barely breathe.
I'm drowning in PR boxes.
Everything's perfect online.

                                                Janie,
                        I'm sure you're too big for me now,
          But am I really the only one who thinks of what ifs?
                          Do you lie awake thinking about
                      That night when the power went out?
                      Just you and me huddled in the sheets.
              I guess if you're ever ready to come home
                            You'll know where to find me.

James,
I miss you.
But I'm scared.
Scared
That if I showed back up in town,
I'd be seen as a failure.
In high school my world was so small
And you occupied every square inch.
If
I knocked on your door,
Would you kiss me like you used to?
Or
Would you see right through me?
I'm too much of a coward to find out,
Because to be rejected by you,
Would mean that I could never love again.

So I'll be a disco-ball instead.
So sparkly, all lit up,
Always reflecting everyone else
So they don't look beyond the surface.
A few thousand followers
But James,
I'd rather follow you.

The Storm

I try to maintain the strength of the sun, but
These bottled-up emotions condensate
And I can't hold back the storm clouds.

Despite my conviction,
The blue turns gray
And a few drops escape my control.

When the drizzles become downpour
The basement floods and ceiling leaks, but
I can't help feeling relieved.

Like a wrung-out sponge
I am wonderfully empty.
The stains on the pavement are drying and
You can finally see the rainbow.

PART 2:

TURBULENCE

The Whole Package

Your embrace is a sigh of relief.
Your kiss whispers silent I love you's
Making my butterflies flutter so fast
They could fly right out of my mouth
And land softly on your hands that
hold the depths of my world.

You're the whole package
Tied neatly in a bow like the strings of your sweatshirt.
You gave shape to this shell of a shameless writer
Your name embossed on my hardback cover.
Words unwritten, written again.
As black meets white the letters are inscribed
Scribbles that ignite flames within my mind.

Nothing is permanent except time
But this time, I intend to get it all on the page.
You're the only thing I want forever
And if the long haul comes too soon
At least running my fingers over this ink—
I can feel you again.

Peonies on the Dining Table

I make the smallest pieces
Seem like the most significant details
Because every part of me is just that important.

Loving me means remembering even the parts I forget.
Like when we walked to brunch the other day and
I said in passing,
"Roses are cliché."

When I came home from work today
There were peonies on the dining table.

Valentine's Day

To the shadow of my mind
The ghost whose hands haunt mine
This one is for you.

~ ~ ~

Today is the 14th of February
I only love ~~this day because of~~ you
What could possibly convey what's in my heart better
Than a kiss?
But, for the first time in 6 years, I can't tell you,
So I write.

~ ~ ~

Thank you
For always
Welcoming me home with a hug
that brings tears to my eyes.
Breaking down my walls
Like the big bad wolf and the house of straw
Leaving my soul bare to you.
But I'm not afraid.
I know I'm your universe
Yet you still let me have my space.
You lift me up
Even when your arms are tired.
You're my end to this game called life.

You made me a morning person.
When I'm on the other side of the bed
Between wake and sleep
You wrap your arms around my waist
And pull me into you
Completing our puzzle masterpiece.
Your blue eyes are my dawn.

~ ~ ~

Sitting on the porch in our rocking chairs,
Hand in hand,
Thinking back on the me who is writing these words,
I smile
At your wrinkled face and
The farm we've built together.
With cows and blueberries
Just like we said we would.
I thank all the gods
That we found each other in this lifetime.
I'll find you again
And the time after that

Because you being there
Is all I've ever known.

Rhode Island

Our love story looks like us running through the halls of
The Breakers.
The only sound the patter of bare feet on tile
As we play hide and seek.
The portraits of past inhabitants watch our smiles fly by
As you chase me to the ballroom,
Sweeping me off my feet in a waltz only we can hear.
The halls haven't felt this alive since the 20s.

Play me a silly song on the tree swing.
Hold my hand in the library before the fire.
Kiss my neck as I watch the rain drop on the windows.
Time stops for the stupidly happy.

Our love breathes shape back into the specters
That walk the halls,
Live in the walls.
Come stroll through the garden, picnic on the beach,
Run after my hat before it hits the water.

Like the sea breeze, comb your fingers through my hair.
You smell like salt and taste like promises
Made under white bedsheets,
It's more intoxicating than the brandy in my glass.

Never leave me.

In my next life

Let me come back as the gold chain that
hangs around your neck,
Let me live forever in the sepia scenes made by sunlight
through stained glass windows.
I don't even need the whole story,
Just this week in this house with you,
Just one more dinner sitting across the table set for twelve.

After that you can close the book and never read it again.
We can become ghosts
Leaving chills of envy
that the tourists can't quite understand.
We'll watch from the roses and laugh
because it's our little secret.
No one but you
And me
At The Breakers.

Dirty

Years of you showing me
That it's normal to crave your hands
Years of you getting me comfortable
With lingerie and candles.
You made it easy.
Peeling off layer by layer
Your eyes alight with adoration.
So sweet and reassuring
Between silk sheets.
I snuggled into vulnerability.

When circumstance came knocking
Threatening to tear us apart
Love was supposed to be the thread
That kept us together.
But threads that spread over oceans
Are sure to snap.
Is a relationship still a relationship
If you can't kiss goodbye?

On the last day of us
Sap-soaked sentences
Made me sticky from head to toe.
Dirty.
Your amber voice flowed through the speaker
Covered my mind.
No matter how much I scrubbed
I'd never be clean.

You punished me
For the things
You taught me were natural.

February 8th

Can't do anything but curl in a ball
Can't stop the tears or my hands from shaking
My head is splitting from the million reasons
Why giving up doesn't make any sense.
But for some reason
I can't bring myself to stay.

For the first time I don't want to use this pain to write something beautiful.
I can't take the blood dripping from the hole in my chest and paint a rose.
All I have left are thorns shaped like questions
    Why couldn't I be stronger?
        Why couldn't I be less selfish?
    Why couldn't we make it work?
        Why couldn't our love be enough?

That last one like shrapnel
Too deep for even surgery to remove.
It will forever catch in my throat
Haunt me every night before bed
Because I fell for you so hard
That I shattered into a million p
                i
                    e
                      c
                        e
                          s.

I can't remember what I used to look like.
I think I was pretty.
Happy.
We fell in love at eighteen
And it's been almost seven years since I've been alone.
You're the only one who can put my fragments back together
But I'm not allowed to love you anymore.

So I'm stuck
Like glue on my fingers
I can't get you off me.

I have to leave all of myself behind and start anew
My best self is reserved for you
I'll keep it polished and shiny
Until you're ready for me again.

My Favorite Lie

Naturally I believed when
you said you'd never lie to me.

But what you said
wasn't true.

You came face to face
with my darkest fear:

> That I couldn't handle distance.

You left me
with the guilt

Of devastating
our perfect story.

To Send You a Text

Swiping through stories on Instagram
I saw a video of you.
I watched it eight times.
You have so many new tattoos.

I wasn't the first one you told.
Was that weird for you, too?

Here I thought I was okay.
I said,
"I think I'm finally ready to reach out
To be just friends."

But seeing your smile
And the way you reached for the camera

I wanted to be that iPhone.
To feel your hand curl around the back of my neck
And pull me in for a kiss
Like you'd done a thousand times before.

I never expected
For you to be an ex.

Today's our anniversary.
Did you think about me?
Did you wonder if I missed you?
Did you go to Fiorella for pasta and
Toast to our broken dreams?

Do you ever go to Mel's and
See our ghosts playing "That's Amore" 8 times on the jukebox?

Maybe in a couple weeks I'll feel better.
Your birthday is coming up.
At least that gives me an excuse
To send you a text.

Happy Birthday

        The
        day
        we
became you and me. Is
honesty even allowed between
us? Instead of telling you, like I
normally would, I write all the
things I wanted to say on your
birthday but didn't: You're the
best person I know. I know
this year hasn't been ideal for either of us.
This time last year I wouldn't have believed
you if you told me that we wouldn't be a
couple right now. I was going to send you
the coolest birthday gift. Probably a new
figurine or tickets to Comic Con. But all you
got from me this year was a poorly-timed
text that lacked my signature sincerity.
I hate having this distance from you physically and emotionally. I want to reach out. Ideally to hold your hand, but I'll settle for just knowing what you're up to. I worry that you don't even want me as a friend. I assume your silence is a reflection that you're still adjusting, and I wish I wasn't the reason for your hurt. Anyway if none of my other wishes come true this year, at least I can give these ones to you: I hope this year is better. I hope it brings you light. I hope you find that new apartment. I hope you fill it with Mario Party and Suzie Cakes. I hope you have fun at our friend's wedding. I hope you find peace. Above all I hope you find someone who won't ever hurt you like I did.

Paper Plane

I wanted to send you a text
In the form of a paper plane.
How do I say I miss you
Without it landing
Like a dagger to the heart?
What words could I say
That would feel like
Walking through smoke's spiderweb trails.
Breezy, but the smell sticks to your leather jacket.

"Hey"
Feels too light
Against the weight of almost 7 years together.
But,
Too many folds and the plane will fall
Flat.

You told me to reach out when I was ready.
But,
Do you still feel the same?
Are you seeing someone else?
Would I be
An inconvenience?
A point of contention?

I'm not even sure how to end this
Because I don't have a clear answer.
Typing the letters

Only to hit erase.
Making origami out of this paper plane.

In this moment,
The only thing I'm sure of
Is that I still love you.

Golden

Well-loved red and white checkered tablecloth
Dull silver cutlery
Barolo in my glass
Warm bread and butter

I imagine you're here.
You think my new hair color is cute and edgy.
Across the table
"What are you having?"
                    Lands on an empty chair.

Memories override reality.
I see your face looking back at me
Eyes full of devotion.
I lean over the candle flame
You place your hand on my face
Comfort.
Peace.

The waiter sets down my caprese.
                I'm eating alone.

I will live forever in my youth
Because that's where you stay.
We grew up together

You are my golden days.

A Cold Night in Paris

Do the rusting locks on the love bridge ever think
Of the hands that once held them
And hope they're well?

When our lock clicked in 2017
I really believed we would open that bakery,
Get married in Utah, have kids
And grandkids.

When we kissed the key and
Hand-in-hand threw it into the Seine
I knew in my heart
We weren't every high-school sweetheart story.
We were forever.
I re-watch that video of us every day.
Our love was more beautiful than Versailles.
Isn't it funny how life changes so swiftly?

12,000 miles, countries apart, and
Unpredictable travel restrictions.
At a certain point I started to question
If you were even real anymore
Or just pixels over FaceTime.

After everything,
Is Paris still your favorite place?
February 14th, 2017
That cold night
I made light

Of all the dead weight of countless locks
Holding onto broken relationships.

And now we're just another one of those sad stories.
If only life was a reflection of what we believed in our gut,
Because boy, did I believe
In you and me.

Forgive Me

Baby, forgive me
I told you I wasn't strong enough.
If you move on without me
I won't argue.
You were always too good for me anyway.

I miss knowing how you really feel.
I miss telling you to get more sleep.
I still feel these things as clearly as this lump in my throat.
Sitting across from someone else at dinner stings.

Tears form in my eyes
His hands down my back
Tears fall down my face.

I'll never forgive myself
For being selfish
For not being what you needed
For not being more.

All the Problems

I'm driving myself crazy trying to understand
Were you really that perfect?
Was I really the villain in our story?
Foot on the gas
For weeks
Speeding through memories
Trying to pinpoint the moment
Where I steered us wrong.

Over dinner with my best friend,
She stops me in my tracks.
"He could've gotten on a plane."

    Maybe she's right.

Maybe she's right again when she says,
"You weren't the only one unwilling to sacrifice."

Maybe I can stop carrying the burden
Of all the problems I thought we didn't have.

San Francisco

I can never go back to San Francisco.
I never loved that city anyway
The confusing cold in the height of summer
The exhausting, never-ending hills.

Regardless,
Every time I think of that place
I have nothing but golden memories.
Just a couple of kids,
Who thought love could overcome anything.

When I play our movie in my head
We're in your bed in that shitty apartment.
I hated the bathroom
And the dust-covered baseboards.
It screamed "College boys live here."
But my favorite conversations happened over pasta
At the Italian place across the street.

I thought if I put us in a frame
And placed it in the best spot in my room
That eventually I would get around
To bringing the real you home for our happily ever after.
But it was never the right time.

I watch the memories burn.
Picnics in Dolores are red and warped
The taste of Ghirardelli is bitter from the smoke

Knowing those ladies at Royal Ground Coffee
Will forget my order
Adds teardrops of gasoline to this fire.

We were supposed to be the strongest.
Everyone looked at us with envy.
They said, "You guys must be the real deal,
If you're still this in love."

But even the perfect couple
Cracked under the pressure.

I wish getting over you was as easy as
Turning six-and-a-half years of memories to ash
In the trash can of my mind.
But I guess I learned that even love
Isn't impervious to time.

Maybe one day I'll be able to go back to San Francisco
And not drive straight to your door.

Light On

purple neon light in your window
are you home?

it's after 2 a.m.
are you still up?

toss a pebble
but you're on the top floor.

should i text you?
you're sending me signals

but i don't have the key
to crack your morse code.

i went to that party
but you didn't show.

were you with someone else?
i keep playing it off.

this game i like.

i should go home
but this december air nips at my heels

a little too much liquid courage
and i'm about to do something stupid

you're the devil on my shoulder—
let's dance.

Ribbon Around My Wrist

Have you ever unraveled a ribbon
Until you get to the cardboard inside?

You unroll and unroll
Silky inch by silky inch
Until there is no more.
Time stops at that precise cut.
Suddenly ungirded and
Hanging by a tiny piece of tape
Must feel lonely.

It's a disappointing realization when all you have
Is what you already passed by.
You could try and reroll the fabric
But it'll only overlap, crooked
Never as pristine as it once was.

I see us in this loose brocade.
My finger running over satin and rough paper,
I only know the you from inches ago.
I wish I could go back to us unwinding those
first centimeters.

Holding the length of my memories with you
Beginnings and middles spooling through my fingertips
I don't know how to let go
And watch this unusable fabric float
To the bottom of a box that

Will just sit in the back of the closet.

I'm not ready to let us collect dust.

I'll take my shiny silver scissors and
Cut a piece from the good times.
Wrap it around my wrist and
Tie it into a neat little bow.
I'll let time weather it
And when it falls off
Maybe then I'll be ready.

Angel

This guy told me I was too perfect.
Untouchable
Like the Sistine Chapel
Not even worth trying.

I get it.
This is punishment.
For ruining the good thing that I had.
Together but never in the same place
An unfinished work of art.
    I wish things were different.
He was the only one who saw me for me
A real person
Not some artist's machination of an angel in oil on canvas.
He loved me regardless of the visible brushstrokes
But the distance between art and audience was too great
So I walked away until things could be ideal.

Now searching for nothing in someone else.
Aren't I what everyone wants?
No strings.
Fantasy isn't always better than reality.
But damn, here I am
Throwing myself at the Meantime and
I'm getting sick of being put on a pedestal.
Screaming behind the glass in this museum that I'm not
just another piece.
I don't want to be out of reach.
Why can't I be the me that everyone else sees?

If he was here
He'd take my face in his hands
Kiss my lips
And tell me that I'm more than enough…

But he's not.

So I'll go handcuff myself back to my quiet little exhibition
Play the part for a while longer
Until I can go back
To him.

Knotted

In my jewelry box
There's a tangle of necklaces.

Layer upon layer of gold chains
So intertwined
That I don't bother.
Instead,
I just place the pendants in the bottom compartment
Beneath the brooches and pearls
Because it's too complicated to try.

You and I are the same.
I won't answer when you ask,
"Are you seeing anyone else?" or
"How do you feel about me?"
I won't take the time
To unravel the difficult questions
Because I'm having too much fun.

I know that this mess won't untangle itself
But I'll let tomorrow deal with that.

Middle Ground

I feel guilty that it's Wednesday night and
I am happy
Sleeping alone
In the center of the bed.

As a woman,
And as a partner,
How do I tell you
That cuddling is nice
But
I need elbowroom?

I don't want to seem brusque
Since we're brand new,
But at this moment
I still love me
More than I love you.

Behind those strong muscles
Is a fragile ego.
In your eyes,
Having a solo date
Equates
To hating time with you.

He says he likes a woman
Who doesn't need a man
But,
I can see you fidgeting

At the sight of a Dior
That I bought myself.

Lest I offend your delicate sensibilities,
I have two options:
Compromise my happiness
Or break it off completely.

Since there is no middle ground

For strong women.

Train Wreck

I don't want to hurt you
But I'm a train off the tracks
And I can't stop.

Every time you brush my hair off my shoulder
Every time you kiss my collarbone
I should pull the brakes
But you're making me forget that they exist.

We make a terrible couple
I hate your crooked teeth and the way you dress.
I hate your immaturity and your laissez-faire lifestyle.
This runaway train is on course for disaster.

Dust is flying
You're ripping off my clothes
I can't see clearly.

We keep chugging forward
Hands in my hair
Your blind hope
My fatalistic grasp of reality.

Red hot coals
Sweat drops down my arms
Eyes roll back in my head
As I feel the final impact.
Bolts and glass flying through the air
Finally it's over
And the end
Tastes like honey.

Alice's Story

As you know, my story starts
On a day like any other
On the bus
Heading to work at the Sunday School.
Looking out the window,
This peculiar feeling is nagging
The one I've had since I was a little girl.
Growing up in Cincinnati
Just never felt like home
But where else would I go?

I had assumed that this was all life had to offer me
Until I met him.
    Cornelius Vanderbilt II.
Have you ever heard a name so beautiful?
The heir to the Central Railroad.
It never mattered to him that I was just a lawyer's daughter
A school teacher.
He saw beyond these things.

When he took me to Rhode Island for the first time
I realized what I'd been missing.
He brought me home;
Bought us a home
Above the cliffs
Where you could hear the waves break
All the way into the house.

When it burned down

The most magnificent maroon color
A piece of me died in those flames.
But reborn was The Breakers only two years later.
Our little wooden home became
The crown jewel of Newport
Draped in red velvet.
We spent the most glorious summers
Chasing chubby little legs across the lawn
And hosting parties befitting the family name.

I never understood how to be Mrs. Vanderbilt.
I've never liked my face in pictures
But Cornelius always thought I was beautiful
And that was enough for me.
Once I became more than Alice,
Everyone wanted something from us.
Cornelius was too good to see the evil in people
So I welcomed the guests
Like a proper wife
But I didn't let just anyone in.

If that made me seem cold
Then that's fine
Because
The best times were spent
With just the family
At The Breakers
Away from it all.

Then I lost him.
I was always telling him that he worked too hard.
That one day, it would all catch up with him.

And then I lost even more.
A mother shouldn't outlive even one of their children
Let alone five.
Living out the rest my days between
New York and Rhode Island,
Even the blue of the Atlantic lost its color.
Nothing motivated me but mourning
I couldn't stand to look at myself in anything but black.
I wished to live in the past.
Shuffle down the halls
Kicking that long four-string pearl necklace,
The last thing he ever bought me.

God,
Did we not do enough?
Was our charity
Our devotion not enough?
All I wanted was to spend my days
Listening to the sounds of the waves breaking on the cliffs
With a man that I truly loved.

I apologize for refusing to come to you
After I passed.
I know if I move on,
I could see him again

And Alfred and Alice and William.
But,
I spent half of my life searching
For what I had been missing.
By the time I found it
I only had a taste.

Allow me to hold on a little longer.

   Haunt these rooms just a little longer.

      Live in denial just a little bit longer.

I'm the worst, but you knew that

Ice blue.
    Cold to the touch.
        Stunning from afar.
            The closer you get the clearer it becomes
                That what lies beneath
                    Is a maelstrom like you've never seen.
I'll laugh at your stupid jokes,
Show you all the things I like about you,
Lay my head on your chest and bat my eyelashes,
Then I'll up and walk away like I wasn't even there to begin with.
No questions asked,
Because I moved on the second we got started.

Didn't you feel my foot halfway out the door during our first kiss?

On this path I've never walked before
Leaving a trail of disaster behind me
Your bed was the warmest I could find at the time.
You deserve better and
I feel bad, I do
But your hands on my body felt so good.
When I closed my eyes
I was with him again.
    His lips on my neck
    His breath in my ear
    His scent on my skin.

I told you I was a hurricane.

My attention the sweetest poison:
Enjoy responsibly.
I'm the Grim Reaper you want to hold hands with.
As you dance circles around my little finger
I'm not even that interested
But you'll keep drinking me down until you're brought to your knees
Begging me to stay.
The most enchanting façade.
But inside I'm just lonely and afraid.
Can't afford to love
But I need to be loved.

Sorry I'm the worst.
If you didn't know then,
At least you know now.

Solo Date

How can I be someone's
perfect someone
when you're definitely not what I need.
Your longing looks are a magnifying glass
and I'm the sizzling ant.

Jumping through fiery hoops
that are progressively shrinking
smaller and smaller.
Each hurdle I can feel the heat singeing hairs on my arms
the clothes on my legs.
For someone who only cares about other people
you're so selfish.

Everything is always about you.
In the middle of work
In the middle of cooking
I drop anything.
When you ask me to listen to your problems
that's a silent promise to give you
my energy
my time
my empathy.

But when I bring up my school stress
or frustration with friends
instead of lending me an ear
you throw your stupid dad jokes
back in my face.

I know it's never your intention
but you're making light
of my heavy heart.
That breach of trust
isolates me.

I'm eating lunch right now
finally alone.
You are nowhere to be found among my thoughts
and it feels incredible to just focus on my salad.

This solo date
is the best I've felt
all week.

Toothpaste

I crossed a line
Understanding the consequences
Of you and I.

They say it's impossible,
To put the toothpaste back in the tube.
But that doesn't mean
I'm not going to try.

My fingers are sticky
Trying to scoop up what we spilled
All over the bathroom counter.

There's no escaping each other,
All of my friends are your friends.
Plus, you're not over me and
You're acting like this mess isn't drying
in the porcelain sink.

You're misinterpreting my words.
Creating conspiracy theories in your head
Falling on the sword
You propped up.
I'm finished
Making excuses for your immature behavior.

Since you're not helping me clean up this mess
I'll just buy a new tube instead
And start again, minty fresh.

The Castle

It's easy for me to build walls
But with you
I built a whole castle.

You encroached on my energy
I added a brick.

You were selfish with my time
Brick.

You threw a tantrum
Brick.

You used me as an excuse to hold yourself back
Seven more bricks.

The reason I built the walls
With such attention and care
Is because being with you
Was like looking into a mirror
At the worst parts of myself.

You brought out all these aspects
That I hate about myself:
The short fuse
The anger
The bitchiness.

Each day together
Another wall was added
To the palace of my growing frustration.

You're toxic.
I don't like the way
Our interactions withered the roses in my palace garden.

So hear ye hear ye,
I'm closing the gate
And filling the moat
With sharp-tongued, sharp-toothed alligators
To distance your kingdom and mine.

Here I thought I was the queen
At denying my own reality
Because of you
I'm a jester.

Atlas Buckled at the Knee

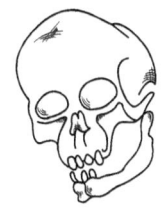

I hold your world in my hands
I fear the weight of your feelings will crush me.

You said I was your favorite dessert
Scoop me up; hold me too tight.

I melt in your embrace
Vanilla ice cream through your fingertips.

Between dusk and dawn
Packed up my car and shut the trunk.

In my rearview mirror you never looked so beautiful.
I was finally free to love you more.

MEMENTO MORI
REMEMBER ME

Jack-in-the-box

The jack-in-the-box
Lives perpetually trapped
Between six cramped walls.

He doesn't understand
Why he cannot breathe with ease.
Why he only feels alive in the brief moment
When he catches the outside air.

When you're stuffed in a box so tightly and
The lever finally cranks that last
teeny
      tiny
            millimeter
You explode into freedom.
Is that what a newborn's first breath feels like?

The immaturity
With which you handle your emotions
Would turn
   and turn
      and turn my lever and
I would wait
   and wait
      and wait
For the time when I could be alone
In the fresh air.

My world became confined to
Those six stuffy walls,
Sealed and welded shut.
I fooled myself into thinking
You understood me,
That my lifestyle was something
You could fit into.

How could I not realize
That I was jack
And you were the box.

Geppetto

Deep bass and pure guitar
Plucking at my heartstrings.
Your hand in mine feels phantom now.
I thought if I cut the threads
I could finally have a mind of my own
But what good is a puppet without its master?
I miss you at the worst times.
My muscles still remember how you used to pick me up
Held me tight
Through the nights
When I thought the sun would never come
But you were the moon to me evermore.

I had to learn how to stand on my own.
The pain in my bare feet on cobblestones
moves me forward.
I'll keep going
Even if the bones start poking through
Because it still feels better than that summer day.
My clothes sticking to my body
I couldn't breathe after
You got bored and tossed me aside.

So I moved up north with the evergreens
To know how to weather any storm.
Your doll runs with wolves now.
You wouldn't recognize me and I like that
With my warpaint and my spears

Wild hair and feral replies
I'm as tall as the aspens and the pines.
I've never been so close to the sky
I am no longer bound by your strings.

Magnetic Properties

You're pulling me in
Positive poles of your personality
Enthralling the negative in me.
My skeleton is vibrating
I can't stop the flow of something this natural.
Every atom in my body is
Drawn to the idea of you.

Drunk

With a voice that tasted like whiskey
"I think we should break up" burned in my chest.
I took it smoothly,
But your indifference tingled my tongue.
I held my head high as I stumbled to my car.
My hands shook when I put the key in the ignition
And drove home drunk
On the pain
Of "we're done."

Allison's Story

Have you ever seen in movies when the rain stops in midair?
It's pouring outside; the hardest rain you've ever seen and then,
    all of a sudden,
        it stops.
As if the sky caught her breath for the briefest instant.

1:45 a.m., September 30th, 2015.
Even through the fog on the window, I could sense the rain outside froze when you walked into the diner for the first time.

One year later
Barefoot on the wood floors
Of my shabby one bedroom apartment
Head in my hands
Wondering
Was it even worth it?

Cracks of lightning outside my window like
The flash on your Polaroid camera.
Takes me back to Cape Town,
Our first getaway.
You held my hands over dinner
And said,
"Allison, I'm going to leave my wife."

The beach never looked so perfect
  Slightly cloudy,

The calm before the storm.
What I failed to realize at the time was that
Every grain of that sand had already been walked over.
Imperfect from the start
But polished enough from being stepped on
To absolutely shine.

I was blinded by what I wished to see in your eyes.
Every word that came out of your mouth
I drank like a castaway with seawater
The most delicious lies.
Was it entertaining watching me slowly lose myself?
After everything
I guess I wasn't enough for you.
You were just stopping by on your drive home and
My coffee was the most
     convenient.

Illicit affairs mean I have no one to talk to
But you.
So what am I supposed to do
Now that you showed me
You never had any intention to leave her
    That I will always come second
        That you never really loved me.

Son of a bitch.

You walked into my life
And now I'm more alone than I've ever known
Hands and knees on the mint green bathroom tiles
Picking up the shattered pieces of my heart.

After the blood from the cuts on my palms
And the tears from my eyes are dried,
I'll stand back up again
Put on my mascara
And go back to the diner

Because my shift starts at 10.
Because that's where we first met.
Because that's where you'll come looking for me,
If you ever wanted to.

I'll probably forever play the fool
When it comes to you.

Antidote

I used to hang onto your words
Nestled in the spaces between syllables
Settled into the meaning I heard.

In reality you constructed a rickety bridge
Each sentence another plank
Tied together with ropes of empty promises.

Today I fell through the rotted wood and
Came close to landing on the jagged rocks below.
I wish I could say it was the first time.

I watch you exhale your drag
As I tend to the cuts on my legs and
I find you no longer enchant me.

My feelings evaporated into the atmosphere and
I felt the weight of you fall off my shoulders
I'm no longer addicted.

PART 3:

THE ARRIVAL

The Difference

I think I finally learned the difference
Between running
                      and
                                          walking away.

Celeste

Yesterday a butterfly landed on my arm
It was the soul of Celeste
A long-passed relative.

She made her presence known
Like when she walked with both feet.
With each flutter of her wings
She told me we were the same,
Cut from the same stubborn silk.
Her strength flowed through my veins and
Quelled the raging waves in my mind.

How did you know
That's what I needed?

Petals of My Past

In the wildest winter I met my childhood self.
Through the haze of blizzard
There she stood
Like a figment of my imagination.
The girl I dream about
Confident, headstrong, secure
The girl I used to be.
She held out her hand
I hesitated
She ran away.
I followed her footsteps up into the mountains.
Along the way she left me pieces of the life I used to know
Petals of my past
The path to my perfection.
A daisy chain to wear as I dance in the snow
A blanket of soft grass when the nights grow cold
A bundle of herbs that bring memories of cooking
with mom.

With each memento
She coaxed me back to her side
To a cozy log cabin at the peak.
She showed me the wall where she etched our inches
"Look how big I've gotten."
We're finally able to see eye to eye.
"Who cares what they think?
If you like it, wear it."
"Don't forget,
Always be nice to Mom and Dad."

Like the braid I made of her mane
We wove together the best parts of ourselves.
Walking down the path into the spring horizon
Her small hand in mine made me feel like
I could do anything.

Daffodil

My dearest Beatrice,

Once upon a time…
Wouldn't that be charming if it's how this started? But no, there is no "Once upon a time." There is only now. We don't exist in yesterday or tomorrow. By that logic, she shouldn't exist either. But she's in the napkins and the forks, in the wallpaper and the carpets, in the azaleas and the rhododendrons. With each breeze that carries the sea, she wanders the halls, seeps into the tea. We'll never be rid of her, and she knew that. Even if we left and set fire to our home, she would always be with us. The blooming scent awakens the memories that keep us wrapped around her finger as if nothing has changed. I long for the cold dead of winter when the snow from his eyes melts and he finally warms to me again. She haunts him but I live for him. She's yesterday and I am today. I am now and what he needs is here. I belong to him and he belongs to me, at least for today. So today, I instructed the gardeners to burn the azaleas and the rhododendrons. I would rather choke on the ash than breathe the sickening scent of her. I think I'll plant daffodils. They're simple and plain and quiet, nothing like Manderley and that suits me fine. I was never Mrs. de Winter anyway.

Sincerely yours,

Puddles

I am the unexplored parts of the sea
You can't imagine the depths I have.
At first glance, I look shallow but,
You have no idea who I really am.

    I am an excellent leader
    I am silly at Disneyland
    I am passionate about food and life
    I am a hopeless romantic
    I am honest, maybe too much
    I am rich with love
    I am one with the universe.

Too bad
You can only see puddles.
Thinking you know all of me.

January

Women who long for wild adventure
Stuck on the treadmill in your apartment gym
I know you.

Reading the words on the page
Can't you feel the sense of familiarity?
I never grew out of believing in fairies and folklore
Where good and bad were as clear as words on the page.

I want adventure and cataclysmic love
I want forgotten châteaux and ruins of villages past
I want sea-stained memories
I want sweltering afternoons in Moroccan coffee houses
With the smell of smoke and cinnamon curled
around my heart.

I would leave this life behind in an instant.
Slip quietly out the back without saying goodbye
like I do at the bar.
Is it selfish to become the daring girl
I've read about in books?
Running my hand over the spines
that contain the hopes for myself,
All I can hear is the call of the wind from distant worlds.

No more monotony or monochrome.
No more going from work to home.
Would you be disappointed if I disappeared?

Yesterday I took one step toward something different.
I bought a boat and named her January.
I had a dream we set sail and landed on the shore
Of a life that was not my own.

Faith

Love is mirrors in a fun house
It takes on many shapes.
Love is not just between family
Or between lovers
But also between
Friends.

Three years ago I met one of the loves of my life.

Moving to Anaheim
Living in the same room with this girl I met online
Beginning our dreams.
Who knew
That those nights across the hall playing rage cage
Would become my most precious memories?

Arms linked running through the park
Shoot to win
You're the Midway Mania Queen
But I scored big.
Good shit never lasts long enough.
I could live forever in those six months.

Counting down to clocking out
Spilling tea
Trading tickets with Sam
For the chance to walk on the Pier at closing
One more time.

My sister from another life
My sister in this life.
We speak in languages unspoken.
Remember that night
I got a little too drunk?

I couldn't help but smile because
I realized that I could be myself.
Crying on the sidewalk
Finally sharing just how stressed I'd been
You helped me get back up
As I knew you would a million more times.

Getting drinks at the airport Chili's
There's no one else.
I swear one of these days I'll settle down
Stop moving around and finally get an annual pass.
You're always my hardest goodbye.

Just a couple more hours 'til midnight and
I'll ride that pumpkin carriage into the fucking ground
If it means we get to have lemonade on the beach
Watching the sun set on our adventures
That we wrote together.

The Art of Performing

A natural born actress
I dazzle the crowd with my witty retorts
"Oh, she's a wonderful young lady."
They applaud my appropriately timed smiles and nods
"Oh, she's lovely."

I play every role:
    Coworker
    Daughter
    Friend
    Lover
    Stranger.

I say my lines with such conviction,
In the moment.
But those come and go
Like scripts and auditions.

You're confused by my contradicting emotions
It was *she* who said, "I love spending time with you."
This me doesn't want anything serious.
You're trying to predict the dialogue
In a movie you've never seen.
But, when the show goes dark
And the makeup comes off
It's a different story.

Walking through the door of my home
I leave my other personalities hung by the door

Without the pressure to perform
I am free to be myself.

I can eat Reese's Puffs for dinner
Dance in my underwear and
Go to sleep as early as I want to.
I can watch my favorite movies over and over
Echo their iconic phrases
Without worrying if someone would find that annoying.

I love being alone.

Like wearing flats that are too tight
Taking them off
You can breathe again.

That's what it means when I tell you I need space.
Don't be offended if I don't answer your texts.
I'm just recharging before I get back on stage
And perform the scenes all over again.

Golden Hour

Something in the warm glow
that falls over the city around 6 o'clock
makes me feel like anything is possible.
Bathed in that golden light
I could go anywhere
be anyone
live any story.

In the background
the soft tones of a trumpet through a gramophone
set the tune
that carries my steps
through a city whose stories
have not yet unfolded.

The old stones and the modern light posts
coming together for a dance that only time can perform.
I am but one of many guests in the crowd
granted a glimpse.
Waiting for the gift of moments
that sweep us off our feet and
allow us to forget the hands on the clock
feel only the familiar hands holding mine.

To love is to live for someone else
for time matters not.

If I Could Build a Man

When it feels like I'll never find you, I like to dream. I like to wonder where you are, what you're doing, what you're reading. I start to fantasize about the adventures we'll have, the places we'll visit. I can't wait to learn everything about you. Even though I like to think that I already know exactly who you are.

Strong.
Like a river stone
Not rough around the edges.
Thoughtful.
Always one step ahead
Don't even bother playing him in chess.
Present.
Conscious of my subtle cues
When I want space.
Driven.
Not tunnel vision
A hustler at heart.

He impresses my mom
Is friends with my dad
Brothers with mine.
Dark brown salty hair
Sun-kissed skin and
Light green eyes.

He kisses my lips
With a soft passion that

Turns me into a pool of melted chocolate
All over the floor.
I've never loved anything more than pasta
But I love him more than *cacio e pepe*.

He likes the way my eyes light up
When I talk about the things I find exciting.
And I like the dimple by his lip
That appears when he talks about his hometown.

His shirt slightly unbuttoned at dinner
I lean over the table
Just to hear his voice
Because it sounds like
The wind in my hair on horseback.

Oops I slipped and fell
Into the river that is his Italian accent
I could float forever on every word.
Especially the ones that sound out
"You look beautiful."

This is what "till death do us part" looks like.
This is what Romeo and Juliet died for.
This is what fairytales are made of.
And that's what you are,

    for now.

Charlotte's Story

The smell of parchment
dry and old
filled with memories and fantasies.
I walked among the bookshelves
replacing misplaced and discarded souls
who are meant for other readers
when I heard the bell at the door,
   "Welcome to Book End!"

I've never seen this man before,
wearing a Loro Piana winter coat.
Definitely out of place for this neighborhood.
Book End doesn't carry anything particularly
special or rare.
I can't fathom what a guy like him
would be doing
here.

I abandon my shelving duties and
make myself available at the counter by the door.
While I wait,
I dive back into this week's adventure.

Apparently I wasn't doing
a very good job of being an employee
since I didn't notice
that he'd been standing at the register
until he cleared his throat.
                      A red heat flared in my cheeks.

I blurted,
    "I'm sorry!" as I hurried to close my book,
    "I didn't see you there.
    Are you all set?"

He wasn't trying very hard to conceal his chuckle,
and I noticed he didn't have a book
    "Can I help you look for something?"

"What are you reading?" he asked.

Since he didn't answer my question,
I will do the courteous thing
and answer his.
    "It's the latest book by Anne Bishop,
    from the *Black Jewels* series."

"It must be good,
if it's stolen your attention so strongly."
                                    Again
                        with the heat in my cheeks.

"I probably shouldn't be reading my favorites at work.
I tend to get a little distracted."

"I'll have what you're having,"
gesturing with his raised eyebrow at my book.

"But you don't even know what it's about."

"I know you like it,
and that's enough for me right now."

Who the hell is this guy?

He's not the first man to hit on me in this bookstore,
But he's definitely the first
to do it like *that*.
Definitely not the standard,
"you're pretty" bullshit.

I don't appreciate
that his tactic
is working.

"Well, since this is the 12th book,
I might recommend starting with the first."

"How about the first three?
I have a lot of catching up to do."

Seriously, who is this guy?

"Sure," I said
a little too enthusiastically
for my taste.
As I came around

from behind the counter,
his eyes followed me,
all the way down the fiction aisle,
and back to the counter.

"That'll be 23 pounds."

He set a 50 on the counter.
I gave him his change and
with a flash of pristine white teeth
he was gone
just the way he came.

Boy, was I wrong
when I thought
that was the last I'd see of
him.

Four weeks and
Two great reads later.
It was 3 o'clock,
the post-lunch lull.
Customers were back at their day jobs
and my afternoon tea was steaming
in my favorite mug.
I decided to retry Homer today and
just as Odysseus was on his way
to the palace of Alcinous,
the bell rang.

I look up from my epic to see
him
again.
Equally as tailored as last time
but in quite a huff.
He stormed up to the counter,

   "What the hell was that?" he exclaimed,
more sad than angry I think.

   "You'll have to be more specific," I gulped.
I'm not really used to dealing with disgruntled customers.

   "I can't tell if you're terrible
   or excellent at your job.
   This book
   was horrible
   and beautiful all at the same time."

I'm not sure what came first,
relief that he wasn't actually angry
or my surprise that he actually read all three books.

                        None of my exes ever
                 read my suggestions before.

I tucked my auburn hair behind my ear and
placed my chin on my hand and said,
   "Which was your favorite?"

"Two.
Hands down.
Watching Saetan with the kids
Oh! and meeting the Kindred,
It took me to places
I never thought I'd go."

With a tender smile,
I recall reading those words
for the first time.
    "That's mine, too."

    With that, time seemed to fly by like ribbon dancers
        emotions flowing and intertwining
        constantly moving and changing shape.
        My whole frame of vision
        filled with purples and reds and oranges and
        like magic melded to create pinks and yellows.
        When I looked up at the clock
        a whole hour had already passed.

He must have noticed
that I checked the clock because he said,
    "I must be keeping you from your work.
    I assume most of your customers
    don't usually stay this long."

    "Normally I would call the cops
    if some guy took an hour to buy a book,

but this happens to be a subject I rather enjoy,
so just this time
I won't call the cops."

"I'm grateful," he said with a light smile.
"Maybe you could
just point me in the direction of book four,
so I can get out of your hair."

Part of me was disappointed
that he was leaving so soon,
but I replied nonetheless,
"Just around the corner there,"
pointing down the fiction aisle.
"Let me know if you can't find it."

"Maybe you could
tell me your name,
in case I get lost."

I huffed a laugh, "Charlotte.
My name is Charlotte."

"Charlotte," he said as if tasting each syllable.

He seemed to savor the sound and
how it rolled off his tongue.
As he turned to walk away,
he pushed back the dark curls

of his lightly styled hair
and under his breath said,
    "Good to know."

Off he went again,
book in hand,
and me,
still confused by our interactions.

        He's just another enthusiastic customer.
                      If that's true,
              Why can't I help feeling
              like I'm reading a story;
        like something I can't see yet
is about to unfold in the next pages?
        Why do I go home at night and
        think about what I should've said
                    or should've done?
        Why is it when I think of his face,
          my bones want me to get up
                      and find him?

Every day for the weeks to come,
My ears stay perked for the sound of the bell.
Each time the door opened
and it wasn't him
I couldn't help my disappointment.

        Who the hell is this guy?

Paradise

Time changes so many things.
Time changes geography and topography
Time changes knowledge and opinions
Time changes relationships and minds.

But, I've always known you, I guess.
Like the butterfly effect and
Like how originally the continents were Pangaea.
Everything is connected.

Isn't it nice to think
That every single step I've taken
Has led me in this direction?
Toward something
Toward someone.
Has it been generations in the making
Leading up to one single afternoon
in a European coffeeshop?

Has the universe been spinning the wheel
On my game of life?
Watching the board from a bird's-eye view?
Picking up one face-down card at a time?

I'm just one of those pink plastic pieces
Every turn
Placing me one step closer.

Time is the greatest murderer
Time is the greatest healer.
Time teaches me to appreciate the beautiful
Time teaches me how to heal from the loss of those moments.

Isn't it nice to think
that at the end of it all
I found my happy ending?
That everything I've gone through
has brought me the one thing
I never knew
I couldn't live without.

you.

PARADISE

**EVERYTHING IS PALPABLE
BIRDS, BEASTS & PLANTS SPEAK THE SAME LANGUAGE**

I Met Fate and He Wore Red

I have this dream.

I'm in a café. The floor tiles are those little black and white hexagons. The furniture is Parisian inspired, you know the ones, those brown plastic wicker chairs with the black and white woven backing. Not the most comfortable but the company of a good book is soothing enough. They serve whole pots of tea here and the staff knows me well. I'm at my usual seat by the window. It's a little bit rainy, the sky has been gray for a couple days now. I don't mind. It sings to the melancholy in me. I've been sucked into my latest novel, called *Dreaming in Europe*, and at this point I don't even notice the people passing by the window or collecting their drinks at the counter. It's not until I go to pour another cup of tea that I notice some scribbles on the napkin near my blue ceramic pot. I delicately unfold the soft paper to find neat, small, handwriting that reads, "I didn't want to disturb you, but maybe sometime you could tell me about what held your attention for so long." Naturally I am shocked and look around to see if the messenger is still in the café. After determining that the culprit fled the scene, my first reaction is to write the whole situation off and lose the napkin forever in the ether that is a woman's purse. Then I notice a phone number next to the note. Very clever, not leaving a name, so I would be intrigued enough to maybe take action. Suddenly, something pulls at me, as if my soul caught on a snag. It whispers to me that this is the moment we've been waiting for. *"Don't let this one pass you by."* I blink and a red fringe flies past my vision. I see a buffalo plaid scarf float down the street on the shoulders of the person I don't know yet. Fate met me in a small café in England. Before I knew it, I add that number and send a text.

This is the story of how we met.

My Love Affair with the Sun

In my bikini
Towel on the ground
Drink you up
Like this sweating iced tea.

That sweet sensation under your rays
Strawberry ice cream
Dripping down my arms.
My reddening skin tingles
Sensitive to the touch.

I'll stay until you're one with the sea
And I need a sweater.
Your kisses on my shoulders
Leave lasting impressions.

At least I have something to remember you by
Until 6 am when I don't have to miss you anymore.

Plot the Course

Leaving home
not for the first time
but this time
for good.
Plot the course to my future.
I have a destination in mind but
it's more like island hopping at this time.
Drop anchor for maybe six months at a time.

The world is just lines on a map
nowhere is out of reach.
But when I meet the end
I want to have lived a thousand lives and
have a thousand stories to tell,
like listening to all the sailors
on all the pirate ships.

I have the best crew.
They bear with me through
all the aimless afternoons and
all the questionable ports.
The currents guide me and
if I'm open to listening
I can hear the wind pulling my sails
in the right direction.

When the masts are splintering
and the helm has my fingerprints engrained,
I'll watch the last sun rise

holding all the seashells
I picked up on the shores
of each precious moment.

The Precipice

Standing on the precipice of my future
I've been here before,
But the view looked different:
Rolling hills and Hollywood trails.

Now I look out onto a canyon labyrinth
These words are my courage.
Am I crazy to jump
Into a future that might be a mirage?

I want to get stronger
And better
At the things that I love.
Could I do this full-time?

I've always been told
Pick a career that makes money
Pick a career that's safe
"You'd make a really good lawyer."

But the one constant in my life has always been
These sentences that I string together.
A side hustle that I never considered
Could make me this happy.

Standing on the precipice.
The wind gently pushing against my back
Nudging me

One step closer.
The background music is building
One step closer.

This time I'm going to listen to myself.

This time I'm going to trust myself.

This time I'm going to jump

    Into the future I make for myself.

Landscape in Ink

My composition comes from the sky.
From the peaks and streaks of cloud.
The negative space against blue and orange sunset,
Form the shape of words and letters.
Raindrops are my ink
Lightning cracks create these scratches.

I bend the energy of the words around me.
From the mountain top
Inspiration flows from my head
Through my roots
Into my fingertips and
Onto the page.

These words are
The product of an afternoon
Spent face to the sky
Soaking in every exquisite molecule.

My Greatest Fear

What's your greatest fear?
Heights?
Spiders?
Loss?

I fear those things, too.
But my greatest fear
Is that one day I will wake up
And have nothing left to give.
That my well will run dry.

I finally found
A direction that excites me
A way for me to live the life I've always wanted.

But what if
This book is just a one-time thing?
Did the oracle ever fear that she would stop seeing?
Or did she have undying faith in her ability?
I've had so many dreams before
All of them came half true.

I want this one for real
The whole dream
At every 11:11
And even at 1:11
I make a wish
On eyelashes

And even eyebrow hairs
That I could keep writing forever
That my pipe dream could come true.

I imagine myself at 35
Sitting by the water
Outside a European café
Surrounded by architectural marvels
And Nutella crêpes
Working on my next hit.

How do you get to be
One of the lucky few
Whose dreams come true?

Confidante

I stood on my tiptoes
to reach the leaves
of the tallest trees.
Told it my secrets.
As my whispers traveled
through
the branches to the roots
I felt safe
surrounded by the kept confessions
of people past.

Garden Walk

Poetry is a garden.
The hedges mark the maze of my mind
Sporting pansies, tulips, jasmine and chrysanthemums
Carefully pruned
Blossoms regardless of season.

Let's take a walk.
Mosey 'round the metaphor magnolias
Smell the familiar scent of shared experiences.
To most, a garden is just a garden
Pretty flowers
And plants they don't care to name
But each word is purposefully placed
Painstakingly cared for.

You will see the seeds I sowed for you.
See dirt drenched fingertips as I typed each letter
Did you find a tree to sit beneath?
Have a picnic and read a book?
A rare flower blooming in the unlikeliest of places?
Those moments, to me,
Are my magic.

Come to terms with the thorns
In the most breathtaking way.
Smile through tears essential for the words you read here.
Surrounded by the peonies, the lilies, the petunias
that I grew
I know I am home.

Poets open their hearts to their readers
Bare our deepest darkest roots
Because we don't know how to live any other way.
Come back anytime.
Underneath might be rough
But above the surface
They bloom the bleeding heart.

Imposter

Reading my hero's words
They coat my soul like a lozenge.
But that minty aftertaste reminds me
That I am different.
My lyrics are not her love poems
And that's good.
I am an imposter
Scribbling away at my misadventures.
She gives me the melody with which
I shape my sentences.
But one day I'd like to stand next to her
And smile.

My Truth

Love shapes me in more ways than one.
No,
I haven't found my special someone.
But,
I have lost someone special.

I write what I feel
I write what I live
I write my truth.

Whatever that truth looks like
In that moment.

I'm only twenty-five
I have three quarters of life left to go.

That's a lot of words
I haven't written yet.
That's a lot of life
I haven't lived yet.

It's exhilarating to know
There are so many more words to go.

Dear Maddie,

There's always good in the bad. I will always be testing you, pushing you past your self-imposed limits, but above all, I will always be here to support you. To guide you in ways that you can't see, and if you listen to my subtle directions, things will always work out. But I need you to believe in yourself and to see the positive when it seems like there is none. Find your inner strength and live with an open mind, and an open heart.

Have fun, don't be too serious, and smile more.

Forever yours,
The Universe.

FIN

Acknowledgments

Writing the acknowledgements is one of my favorite parts of publishing. It gives me the chance to reflect on how truly blessed I am by the people in my life. *What I Gave You* wouldn't be here without all the people and the experiences that the universe gave me.

When I set out to write this book, my biggest goal was to improve as a poet, and I couldn't have done it without the help of the team at the Creator Institute and at New Degree Press. You took my raw, messy poems and helped me polish them into something I am incredibly proud of. Thank you for your immense efforts and patience.

I want to give a special thank you to Konstantin Bessmertny. This book feels like my first creative debut and to be able to work with someone of your talent was an absolute dream. Thank you for your encouragement and words of advice. Thank you for taking my poems and bringing them to life with your art.

To my mom and dad, thank you for always being there to champion my ambitions and goals. I am the luckiest girl in the world to have parents like you. To my big brother, who has always pushed me to be the best version of myself, thank you. I am so proud to be your sister and I will never stop improving and never stop being curious. Thank you to all my friends, I love you more than I can say. Thank you for being in my life even if I'm not always physically present. Knowing you are there in spirit gives me the strength to weather any storm.

Last, but not in any way the least, thank you to all my early readers. Your feedback and positive comments made my heart so full. All I wanted was to share my experiences with the world in the hopes that it would make just one person feel seen. Knowing that my words have resonated with you in the smallest way brings the biggest smile to my face. I had so much fun putting this little book together and I can't wait to keep creating more for you. All I can say is, this is just the beginning.

www.ingramcontent.com/pod-product-compliance
Lightning Source LLC
LaVergne TN
LVHW011836060526
838200LV00053B/4056